Translated & Edited by

L. CLARK KEATING

& ROBERT O. EVANS

An Introduction to English Literature

Jorge Luis Borges

In collaboration with
María Esther Vázquez

The University Press of Kentucky

Título del original en castellano:
Introducción a la literatura inglesa
Publicado en Buenos Aires, República Argentina,
por Editorial Columba
© by Columba S.A.C.E.I.I.F.A. 1965

ISBN: 0-8131-1307-5

Library of Congress Catalog Card Number: 73-86401

Editorial and Sales Offices: Lexington, Kentucky 40506

Contents

Translator's &
Editor's Preface

This slim volume, sixty-five pages in Spanish, bears the
the names of both Jorge Luis Borges and María Esther
Vázquez without distinguishing the contributions of
either. However, it is surely no discredit to Miss Vázquez
to say that the book contains much the same stylistic
flavor as Borges's *An Introduction to American Literature,* to which this volume is meant to be a companion.

To introduce English literature in sixty-five pages is of
course a difficult task. English literature, the pride of the
English-speaking peoples, as Winston Churchill would
name them, has enjoyed the best efforts of literary historians at least since the time of Taine. Borges in his own
Brief Bibliography acknowledges some of them: Andrew
Lang, Emile Legouis and Louis Cazamian, George Saintsbury, George Sampson; and no doubt he has read them
all carefully and with relish. His little volume deserves a
place beside these grander compendiums.

For the American literature book the translator-editor

claimed attention because it presents American literature by an outsider who loves both literature in general and that of the United States as he sees it, but no such claim can be made for the volume on English literature. English literature, much more venerable and better known, has been for a long time a worldwide possession rather than the exclusive property of those who speak the language, and as such it is loved and venerated wherever there are cultured people. It is out of such love that Borges and his collaborator have produced a brief Spanish abridgement, as an introduction for students in Argentina. But, as may be said of everything to which Borges has put his hand, the volume has merits far beyond its immediate purpose, for it communicates not only the author's great love for English culture and literature, and that with a distinct charm, but also his remarkable erudition. No one upon reading this book can doubt that Borges has read every one of the authors he mentions not only with a clear and critical insight but with joy as well. Charm, Borges reminds us, is, according to Robert Louis Stevenson, the supreme criterion of literature, and how well he exemplifies that quality in this work.

This is, then, a charming book. It is also very accurate, not only in the facts that it catalogs but also in the judgments that it makes. There are nonetheless some indications here and there of the author's personality and tastes. He is a little hard, for example, on Carlyle probably because Carlyle's view of history, as the product of great men, served to encourage the predecessors of the Nazis. Shelley and Walter Scott are apparently not among his favorites, though such a short book must of course be highly selective. On the other hand, the reader cannot miss his delight with Chesterton, to whom he refers more often than to any other source.

We are also provided with an understandable (and often useful) Spanish, and particularly Argentine, frame of reference, though Borges's comparisons extend far beyond writers in his native tongue. That is to say, the French and Germans have their day, too, for the author, as one of the true intelligentsia of the world, knows them all intimately. But if Borges is an extremely well-read man, he is also a witty one; though the wit that appears here usually comes from what he has selected for us, as, for example, when he reminds us that Andrew Lang said of William Morris's *The Tale of Beowulf,* with its intention of translating the poem into a modern, Germanic idiom, that it turns out to be more archaic than the original.

The *Introduction to English Literature* is organized differently from the companion volume, and perhaps more conventionally: by centuries, by prose, by poetry, and by movement. It neglects, because of the size of the undertaking, some of the delightful though minor subjects, such as the detective story or science fiction, which Borges found time to mention in the other work. But at the same time it provides in an effortless fashion a good deal of minor information on major subjects that is not found in the grander literary histories. This is part of the charm and value of the book, which unlike most brief summaries can be read with enjoyment from the first page to the last.

As translators we have attempted to render insofar as possible the flavor of the Spanish style, and as editors to footnote the rare lapses that have crept into the Spanish text. Titles have been standardized generally in accord with forms in *CBEL*. We have added what seemed to us to be a minimal number of footnotes mostly for explanation. No doubt the notes contain very little that Borges could not have included himself had he seen fit to do so. With that admission, wrung from the fact that footnotes to a great man will never possibly suit everyone, we conclude what has been a labor of love and indeed a pleasure.

Lexington, 1974

Author's Preface

To abridge the history of one of the richest of literatures within the brief compass of this book is an obviously impossible undertaking. Three imperfect solutions suggested themselves: first, to disregard proper names and attempt to sketch the general outline of its development; another possibility was to pile up names and dates in an exhaustive manner, from the eighth century to our own; or, finally, to seek out the representative authors and works of each period. We have chosen the last-named procedure. Novalis wrote that every Englishman is an island, and this insular character has made the work more difficult; since British literature, in contrast to French, consists, above all, of individuals rather than of schools. It will be easy to find omissions on the following pages. However, they do not imply disdain, forgetfulness, or ignorance.

Our essential purpose has been to interest the reader and to stimulate his curiosity to a deeper study.

In the bibliography we have indicated the most readily accessible sources.

Buenos Aires, 19 April 1965

[*1*]

The Anglo-Saxon Period

Of all the vernacular literatures which developed during the Middle Ages on the fringe of literature in Latin, that of England is one of the oldest. To put it another way, there are few other texts that can be attributed to the end of the seventh or the beginning of the eighth centuries of our era.

The British Isles were a Roman colony, the least protected, and most northern one of the vast empire. The native population was of Celtic origin. By the middle of the fifth century the Britons professed the Christian faith, and Latin was spoken in the cities. Then disintegration of the Roman power structure occurred. According to the chronology established by the Venerable Bede, the Roman legions abandoned the island in 449. From north of Hadrian's wall, which corresponds approximately to the border between England and Scotland, the Picts, Celts who had not been conquered by the empire, invaded the country and laid it waste. On the southern and western coasts the island was exposed to depredation and pillaging by Germanic pirates, whose ships sailed out of Denmark, the Low Countries, and the mouth of the Rhine. Vortigern, a king or chief of the Britons, thought that the Germans would be able to defend the country from the attacks of the Celts; and so, according to the custom of the times, he sought the help of mercenaries. The first of these were Hengist and Horsa, who came from Jutland. Other Germans followed them, the Angles, Jutes, and Saxons, the first of whom gave their name to the land: England (Angleland).

The mercenaries routed the Picts, but they allied themselves to the pirates, and in less than a century they had conquered the country, where they founded small, independent kingdoms. Such Britons as had not been butchered or reduced to slavery sought refuge in the rocky fastnesses of western Gaul where their descendants still remain in that part of France which, ever since, has borne the name of Brittany. The churches were sacked and burned. It is curious to observe that the Germans did not establish themselves in the cities, which were too complex for their minds or whose phantoms perhaps they feared.

To say that the invaders were German is to say that they belonged to the stock which Tacitus described in the first century of our era and which, without achieving or desiring political unity, shared kindred customs, mythologies, and languages. Since they were men from the North or Baltic Sea, the Anglo-Saxons spoke a language midway between the west German languages, that is, old High German, and the various Scandinavian dialects. Like German and Norwegian, Anglo-Saxon, or Old English (the terms are synonymous), had three grammatical genders and its nouns and adjectives were declined. Compound words abounded, a fact that had an influence on their poetry.

In all literatures poetry antedates prose. Anglo-Saxon verse lacked rime and was not composed of a set number of syllables. Stress in the line usually fell upon three words which began with the same sound, a pattern known as alliteration. An example of this is "wael spere windan on tha wikingas," which means "throw the lance of destruction at the Vikings." Since epic themes were always the same, and as the necessary words were not always alliterative, the poets had recourse to compounds. In time it was discovered that such periphrasis could be metaphorical,[1] and so they said *whale road,* or *swan road* for "the sea," and *a meeting of spears* or *meeting of anger* for "a battle."

Historians of literature customarily divide Anglo-Saxon poetry into pagan and Christian, and this division is not totally misleading. Some Anglo-Saxon poems allude to the Valkyries; others sing the deeds of Judith or those of the apostles. The works with Christian themes sometimes have epic traces, that is to say, pagan elements. Thus, in the justly famous *The Dream of the Rood* Jesus Christ is "the young warrior who is the All powerful God." In another place the Israelites who are crossing the Dead Sea receive the unexpected name of Vikings. A different sort of division seems to provide more clarity. A first group of poems would therefore correspond to those which, although written in England, belong to the common Germanic stock. Also, it should not be forgotten, that the Christian missionaries everywhere, except in the Scandinavian regions, blotted out all traces of the ancient mythology. A second group, which we might call insular, is that of the so-called elegies. In these are to be found the nostalgia, the loneliness, and the passion for the sea [2] which are typical of England.

[2]

The Fourteenth Century

Two historic events of equal importance changed and finally disrupted ancient England. Beginning in the eighth century the Danes and Norwegians harassed the coasts of England and settled in the north and center. And in the year 1066 the Normans, a people of Scandinavian stock but of French culture, conquered the whole country. Thereafter, the priests spoke Latin and the court French, while the Anglo-Saxon language, divided into four main dialects, and full of borrowed Danish words, was relegated to the lower classes. For two centuries there was no native literature, but a resurgence occurred after 1300. By then the language was no longer the same. Common words, as at present, were generally Germanic. Those which had to do with culture were Latin or French. Then a curious phenomenon occurred. Anglo-Saxon had disappeared, but its music was still in the air. Men who had not been able to decipher *Beowulf* composed long poems in alliterative meter.

The most famous of these is *The Vision concerning Piers Plowman,* which is more than six thousand lines long. It is impossible to narrate the plot, for it concerns various stories that dissolve into each other like the images of a kaleidoscope. In the beginning we see "a fair field full of folk." At one end there is a subterranean prison, which is hell, at the other a tower, which is heaven. Piers Plowman suggests to the others a journey to a new sanctuary, that of Truth. Gradually the seeker is confused with the object of his quest. The fight with the Demon is presented in the medieval form of a tournament. Piers arrives riding on a donkey, and one of the spectators asks: "Is this Jesus the Jouster, whom Jews killed, or is it Piers Plowman? Who painted him so red?" Suddenly the vision dissolves; the Demons, Satan, and Beelzebub, who are distinct characters, defend hell with their artillery against the siege of Jesus. Satan in *Paradise Lost* will use the same means. The Demon refuses to release the souls condemned for eternity. A mysterious woman argues that if Satan took the form of a serpent to deceive Eve, then God may well assume the form of man. It is also said that if God took human form he did so in order to know in an intimate way the sins and wretchedness of humanity. The poem has been attributed to William Langland who, under the nickname Long Will, appears as a character in the text.

In *Sir Gawayne and the Grene Knight* we have a paradoxical union of Saxon meter and Celtic theme. The story belongs to what was called in the Middle Ages *Matter of Britain,* that is, the cycle about King Arthur and the Round Table. On Christmas Eve a green giant, riding a gigantic green horse appears before the king and his knights, ax in hand, and asks them to cut off his head, with the proviso that at the end of a year and a day the man who decapitates him must come to seek him in an unknown and distant Green Chapel, there to be sub-jected to an identical test. No one wants to accept the challenge. Arthur, to save his honor, is on the point of taking the ax when young Gawayne seizes it and decapi-tates the giant. The latter picks up his head and leaves, and the head repeats that within a year and a day he will expect Gawayne to come. The year passes. The poet describes the seasons, the snow, the new roots. Gawayne sets out on the long and hazardous road, leaving moors and mountains behind him. An old knight and his wife, a woman more beautiful than Queen Guinevere, receive him and give him hospitality. Three times the knight goes out hunting; three times the woman tempts Ga-wayne, who resists; but he does accept from her a green girdle embroidered in gold. On Christmas day he comes upon the chapel. A sword descends upon Gawayne, but the heavy iron hardly leaves a mark on his neck. This is the reward for his chastity; the slight mark is the penalty for having accepted the green girdle. The poem, whose author is unknown,[7] has more than two thousand allitera-tive lines and it brings together chivalric ideals and a grotesque and fantastic imagination.

We now come to Geoffrey Chaucer (1340–1400), called by many the father of English poetry. This is by no means an exaggeration, although the poets of the Saxon epoch preceded him. The poets and the language they used have been forgotten, while the great lines of Chaucer are not essentially different from those of Milton or Yeats. Shake-speare read them. Wordsworth translated them into modern English. Chaucer was a page, soldier, courtier, member of parliament, member of what today we would call the secret service, diplomat in the Low Countries and in Italy, and finally inspector of customs. French, Latin, and up to a certain point Italian were familiar to him. Among his works are a treatise on the use of the astrolabe,[8] dedicated to one of his sons, and a version of the *Consolation of Philosophy* by Boethius. A French colleague hailed him with the title of the great translator. Translation during the Middle Ages was not a philological exercise accomplished with the aid of a dictionary (of which there were none); it was an aesthetic recreation. This single example will suffice to show that Chaucer was a great poet. Hippocrates had written "ars longa, vita brevis." Chaucer translated this saying, "The lyf so short, the craft so long to lerne." Thus, the dry Latin observation is transformed by Chaucer into a melancholy meditation.

Influenced by the *Roman de la Rose*[9] he began by composing allegories, and it is typical of Chaucer that one of his first, *The Book of the Duchesse,* intended as a lament upon the death of the Duchess of Lancaster, includes humorous references to the poet himself. To the same period belongs also his *Parlement of Foules.*

Chaucer's most profound book, although it is not his most famous, is the slow moving narrative poem *Troilus and Criseyde.* The plot and a third of the stanzas are taken from Boccaccio, but Chaucer has changed the characters and has made, of Pandarus, for instance, who in the original was a young libertine, a middle-aged man who hands over his niece Criseyde to the clandestine amours of Prince Troilus while at the same time abounding in lengthy moral preachments. It has been said that this tragic story, which has the siege of Troy for its setting, is the first psychological novel in European literature. We quote a few lines from the fifth book, at once passionate and rhetorical. Troilus rides by the house of Criseyde, whom he has abandoned, and speaks thus:

> "*O palace desolate,*
> *O house of houses whilom best ihight,*
> *O palace empty and disconsolate,*
> *O thou lantern of which quaint is the light,*
> *O palace, whilom day, that now art night,*
> *Well oughtest thou to fall, and I to die,*
> *Since she is went that wont was us to gye!*
>
> . . . .
>
> *Yet, since I may no bet, fain would I kiss*
> *Thy cold doors, darst I for this route;*
> *And farewell shrine, of which the saint is out!"*

Chaucer began many poems. The only one that he finished was *Troilus and Criseyde,* which is more than eight thousand verses long.

By the year 1387 Chaucer had accumulated many un-published manuscripts. He decided to gather them to-gether in a volume, and thus the famous *Canterbury Tales* was born. In similar collections, *The Thousand and One Nights,* for instance, the stories have nothing to do with the person who tells them. In the *Canterbury Tales* they serve to illustrate the character of each narrator. Some thirty pilgrims, representing the various social classes of the Middle Ages, set out from London toward Beckett's sanctuary.[10] One of them is Chaucer, whom his fellow pilgrims, his invented characters, handle roughly. A tavern keeper, who serves as a guide, proposes that to lighten the tedium of the journey the pilgrims should tell stories, and the person telling the best one will be re-warded with a dinner. After thirteen years of working at it, Chaucer left this vast work unfinished. It contains contemporary English stories, Flemish stories, classical tales, etc. Also in it is a story that appears in *The Thousand and One Nights*.

Chaucer introduces into English poetry the measured and rimed verse that France and Italy had taught him. On a certain page he makes fun of alliterative verse, which doubtless seemed to him a rustic and antiquated process. He was deeply preoccupied with the problem of predestination and free will.

Chesterton wrote an excellent book about him.

[3]

The Theater

At the beginning of the Christian era the Church condemned the arts, which were linked, naturally, to pagan culture. For this reason it cannot but seem paradoxical that during the Middle Ages the theater was reborn from the liturgy. The mass represents the Passion; the Sacred Writings abound in dramatic episodes; and, for the edification of the faithful, the clergy staged some of these. From the sanctuary they moved out to the churchyard and from Latin into the vernacular languages. Thus were born the miracle plays which in France and Spain were called mysteries. In England the guilds dramatized the whole Bible and tried to depict universal history in the open air—from the fall to the judgment. These dramatic presentations, which lasted several days, were generally put on in May.[11] Sailors manned Noah's Ark, shepherds brought sheep, and cooks prepared the Last Supper. From miracles the drama turned to Moralities, that is to say, to plays of an allegorical character, whose protagonists are vices and virtues. The most famous of these is *Everyman*.

As the religious theater gave way to the secular, the first illustrious name is that of Christopher Marlowe

(1564-1593).[12] The son of a Canterbury shoemaker, he belonged to the group of *University Wits* who competed with the professionals to whom the companies had entrusted the production of plays. He is alleged to have frequented the famous School of Night which met at the home of the historian and explorer Sir Walter Raleigh. Marlowe was an atheist and blasphemer. He served as a spy, and at twenty-nine he died of a stabbing in a tavern. An American critic has even attributed the works of Shakespeare to him. He invented what Ben Jonson called the mighty line. In each of his tragedies there is, perforce, a single protagonist, the man who defies moral laws: Tamburlaine seeks the conquest of the world; the Jew Barabbas, gold (in *The Jew of Malta*); Faustus, the sum of Knowledge. This all corresponds to the epoch ushered in by Copernicus, who proclaimed the infinity of space, and Giordano Bruno, who visited the School of Night and who was burned at the stake.[13]

Eliot observes that in Marlowe hyperbole is always on the point of falling into caricature, but never quite does so. The same observation could be applied to Góngora and Hugo. Tamburlaine, in the tragedy that bears his name, appears in a carriage to which have been harnessed four kings, his prisoners, whom he curses and whips. In another scene he imprisons the sultan of Turkey in an iron cage; and in another he throws into the flames the Koran, the sacred book, which for Marlowe's spectators may well have appeared to stand for the Bible. In addition to the conquest of the world, a single passion rules his breast, his love for Zenocrate. The latter dies, and Tamburlaine understands for the first time that he too is mortal. Now mad, he orders his soldiers to arm their artillery against heaven and to emblazon the firmament with black flags to signify the slaughter of the gods. Less worthy of Tamburlaine than of Faust seem these words that Marlowe puts into the mouth of the former and which are characteristic of the Renaissance: "Nature has created our souls to understand the prodigious architecture of the world."

The Tragical History of Dr. Faustus was praised by Goethe. The protagonist makes Mephistopheles bring him the ghost of Helen. In ecstasy he exclaims: "Was this the face that launched a thousand ships, And burnt the topless towers of Ilium. Sweet Helen, make me immortal with a kiss!" In contrast with Goethe's Faust, Marlowe's is not saved. He sees the sun of his last day declining and cries: "See, see where Christ's blood streams in the firmament. One drop would save my soul, half a drop." He wants the earth to hide him; he wants to be a drop of the ocean, a speck of dust. The clock strikes twelve; the demons bear him away. "Cut is the branch that might have grown full straight, And burned is *Apollo's* Laurel bough, That sometime grew within this learned man."

Marlowe foreshadows the advent of Shakespeare, who was his friend. He gave to blank verse a splendor and a flexibility never before known.

The destiny of William Shakespeare (1564-1616) has been judged mysterious by those who look upon him from outside his epoch. In reality there is no mystery. His times did not pay him the idolatrous homage that ours do for the simple reason that he was a writer for the theater, and the theater was in those days a subordinate branch of literature. Shakespeare was an actor, an author, and an impresario. He frequented the gatherings of Ben Jonson, who years later would deplore his "little Latin and less Greek." According to the actors who dealt with him, Shakespeare wrote with supreme facility and never blotted a line. Ben Jonson, like a good literary man, could not refrain from remarking: "I wish he had blotted a thousand." Four or five years before he died Shakespeare retired to his village, Stratford-on-Avon, where he acquired a house that was evidence of his new prosperity and devoted his time to lawsuits and loans. Glory did not interest him; the first complete edition of his works is posthumous.[14]

The theaters, located in the suburbs (mostly in Bankside across the Thames) were unroofed. The public, or groundlings, stood in a central courtyard. All around were galleries, which were somewhat more expensive. There was no fly or curtain. The people of the court, accompanied by their servants who brought chairs for them, occupied the sides of the stage, and the actors had to make their way past them. In the drama of today, a conversation already begun can continue when the curtain rises. In Shakespeare's day, the actors had to come on stage. For the same reason, lack of a curtain, they had to carry off dead bodies, which were customarily abundant in the last act. It was for this reason that Hamlet was buried with full military honors. Four captains bear him to his grave and Fortinbras says:

> *And, for his passage,*
> *The soldier's music and the rites of war*
> *Speak loudly for him.*

The absence of flies, fortunately for us, led Shakespeare to use words to describe his scenes. More than once he did so for psychological reasons, also. King Duncan sees the castle of Macbeth, where they will murder him one night, looks at the tower and swallows flying, and observes with pathetic innocence, foreign to his destiny, that where they nest "the air is delicate." [15] Lady Macbeth, however, who knows that she is going to kill the king, says that the very crows grow hoarse as they announce the entrance of Duncan. "And when goes hence?" she asks. "To-morrow, as he purposes," replies Macbeth. "O, never/ Shall sun that morrow see!" she answers. (1.5. 60–63)

Goethe thought that all poetry is circumstantial, and it is not impossible that Shakespeare was led to write the tragedy of Macbeth, one of the most intense creations in all literature, by the fact that the theme was Scottish and that a king of Scotland, James I, was occupying the throne of England. As for the three witches, or fates, it is not out of place to recall that the king had written a treatise on witchcraft and believed in magic.

More complex and slower in pace than *Macbeth* is the tragedy of *Hamlet*. The original argument is to be found in the pages of the Danish historian Saxo Gramaticus, whom Shakespeare did not read directly. The character of the hero has been the object of countless discussions. Coleridge attributes to him a primacy of imagination and intellect over willpower. In a sense there are no secondary characters. But we may recall Yorick, created forever by a few words of Hamlet, who holds his skull in his hands. Similarly unforgettable are the two women protagonists of the tragedy, Ophelia, who understands Hamlet and dies abandoned by him, and Gertrude, his mother, harsh, tortured, and sensual. Furthermore, there also occurs in

Hamlet an enchanting device, a play within a play, which was praised by Schopenhauer and which would have pleased Cervantes. In both tragedies, *Macbeth* and *Hamlet,* a crime is the central theme; the first was motivated by ambition, the second by ambition, vengeance, and a need for justice.

Far different from the two works just mentioned is Shakespeare's first romantic tragedy, *Romeo and Juliet.* Its theme is far less the final misfortune of the lovers than the exaltation of love. As always in Shakespeare there are curious psychological intuitions. The fact that Romeo is on his way to a masked ball in search of Rosaline when he falls in love with Juliet has been praised and admired. His soul was ready for love. As in Marlowe, the frequent exaggerations are always justified by passion. Romeo sees Juliet and exclaims: "O, she doth teach the torches to burn bright!" As in the case of Yorick, already mentioned, we meet characters who are revealed to us in a very few words. The plot requires the hero to obtain a poison. The apothecary refuses to sell it to him. Romeo offers him gold and the apothecary says: "My poverty, but not my will, consents." And Romeo replies: "I pay thy poverty and not thy will."

In the farewell scene in the bedroom, the atmosphere itself intervenes as a psychological element. Both Romeo and Juliet wish to delay their separation; the beloved woman wishes to persuade her lover that the nightingale has sung and not the cock which announces the morning; and Romeo, whose life is at stake, is willing to accept the idea that the dawn is but a gray reflection of the moon.

Another drama of romantic character is *Othello, the Moor of Venice,* whose themes are love, jealousy, pure evil, and what the jargon of our century has decided to call an inferiority complex. Iago, who hates Othello, also hates Cassio, who holds a military rank higher than his own. Othello feels inferior to Desdemona because he is many years older than she; and she is a Venetian, while he is a Moor. Desdemona accepts her fate and is assassinated by Othello, after she has tried to take upon herself the blame for her own death. Love and fidelity to her lord define her. When Iago's vile strategem is found out, Othello recognizes her virtues and stabs himself, not for remorse, but because he discovers that he cannot live without her.

The limits imposed by this outline do not permit a mention of important works such as *Antony and Cleopatra, Julius Caesar, The Merchant of Venice,* and *King Lear.* We should like, however, to allude to the character of Falstaff, a ridiculous but lovable knight like Don Quixote, but who differs from the latter in the fact that he has a sense of humor, a quality quite out of character in the literature of the seventeenth century.

Shakespeare also left a series of one hundred forty odd sonnets.[16] They are, without doubt, autobiographical, and allude to a love story that no one has entirely succeeded in unraveling. Swinburne calls them "divine and dangerous documents." One of them includes a reference to the neoplatonic doctrine of the "world soul," others to the Pythagorean doctrine that universal history is repeated cyclically.

The last play that Shakespeare wrote was *The Tempest.* Ariel and his opposite Caliban are extraordinary inventions. Prospero, who destroys his magic book and renounces the arts of magic, may well symbolize Shakespeare's farewell to his creative labors.

[4]

The Seventeenth Century

From this century, which is no less rich in literary than in historical events, we choose three very different writers: Donne, Browne, and Milton. Before doing so a few words must be said concerning *The New Atlantis,* which is the first example of scientific fiction in universal literature.[17] It was written by the philosopher Francis Bacon (1561–1626). It describes some travelers who reach an imaginary island not far from Peru. The island is full of laboratories in which rains, snows, rainbows, and echoes are produced, and where music is preserved by mechanical means and pictures of ceremonies and battles are artificially projected. There are shipyards producing ships which travel through the air or under the water. There are apples the very fragrance of which has curative powers. There are botanical and zoological gardens which develop through cross-breeding all possible species.

The fame of John Donne (1573–1631) has suffered long periods of eclipse. Forgotten at his death, he was rediscovered by the romantic writers of 1798. Today he is considered one of the great poets of England. He was present at and perhaps took part in the sack of Cadiz by the cor-

Nativities and Deaths with equall lustre, nor omitting Ceremonies of bravery, in the infamy of his nature."

More famous, but not superior to the preceding, is John Milton (1608–1674). He was a poet, theologian, polemist, and dramatic author. An ardent republican, he was Latin Secretary to Cromwell, which is the same as saying that he was in charge of foreign affairs, since Latin was at that time the language of diplomacy. In his tenacious execution of his official tasks he was not deterred by the fear of blindness, to which he finally succumbed. He was married twice and was in favor of divorce and polygamy. In Italy he became acquainted with Galileo, and the image of the moon, as seen through his telescope, will reappear much later in his description of the shield of Satan in *Paradise Lost.* He wrote verse in Latin and Italian, and one of his first works was a direct translation of the Psalms. He justified the beheading of Charles I. When Charles II ascended the throne he was handed a list of regicides, but the king pushed it aside, declaring that his hand was incapable of signing death sentences.

Before he had written a single line John Milton knew that he was predestined to be a poet. He wished to leave a book such that the world "should not willingly let it die." He thought that in order to sing of heroic actions one must have a heroic soul. For this reason like a priest of poetry he remained chaste until the day of his marriage, despite his sensual temperament. In the seventeenth century the primacy of Homer was unassailable. From the conviction of his preeminence, perhaps a correct one, he decided that the Homeric genre or epic was greater than any other. Milton prepared himself, therefore, to write a great epic. He studied the world's most famous works in their original languages, and from so doing he reached the conclusion that Hebrew literature was superior to Greek and Greek to Latin. In the same fashion he thought that rime was a poor modern invention, unknown or disdained by the ancients. All he needed was to choose a theme for his work. The cycle of the Round Table fascinated him, but Charles I, whose execution Milton had approved, believed himself to be a descendant of Banquo, who, according to tradition, was a descendant of King Arthur. Obviously this theme was not suitable for a republican. It was also ruled out for another reason. King Arthur was a Celt, and in the seventeenth century the English, and especially the republicans, began to recall that they were of Germanic stock. What theme to choose, then? For Milton, as for Torquato Tasso, the *Iliad* suffered from a single defect.[19] The siege and fall of Troy was not thought to be of interest to all men. The Old Testament suggested to him a more ample subject: the creation, the wars of the angels, and the sin of Adam. In 1667 Milton, now blind, published *Paradise Lost*.

The sublime tone is typical of Milton, but the reader is not long in feeling that there is much that is mechanical in the poem, since it is not motivated by passion.

Samuel Johnson, the most authoritative of the English critics, wrote in the eighteenth century that *Paradise Lost* is one of those books that the reader admires, abandons, and does not continue reading. "None ever wished it longer than it is. Its perusal is a duty ratther than a pleasure. We read Milton for instruction, retire harassed and overburdened, and look elsewhere for recreation; we desert our master and seek for companions." Satan, who wars against Omnipotence, has been adjudged by many to be its real if unnamed hero.[20]

Samson Agonistes, published in 1671, is perhaps Milton's masterpiece. A tragedy in the classic mode, the violent deeds occur offstage while the chorus comments on them. It includes splendid verses. Samson, betrayed by his wife, surrounded by his enemies and blind, is a mirror image of Milton.

For a long time Milton was looked upon as a typical Puritan. The posthumous discovery of his theological manuscript, *De Doctrina Christiana,* reveals him as a heretic, as far from Calvin as from Rome, and inventor of a system that borders on pantheism. Denis Saurat has discovered in this volume the influence of the *Cabbala.*

[5]

The Eighteenth Century

Beyond the names of authors and works, two contrasting events may be said to define this century. The first, corresponding to the first half, is classicism, or neo-classicism, which is to say the organization of prose and verse according to the norms of reason and clarity as represented by Boileau. The second, which is much more important, is the romantic movement which, just before the middle of the century, arises in Scotland with James MacPherson[21] and is then diffused through England, Germany, France, and finally in all the western world, not excluding Argentina.

To exemplify the first, we might choose, insofar as poetry is concerned, Alexander Pope; in prose, Joseph Addison or the bitter Jonathan Swift. We select instead the great historian Edward Gibbon (1737–1794).

He was of ancient although not illustrious stock. One of his ancestors during the Middle Ages was the *marmorarius* or architect of the king. Gibbon was born in the vicinity of London. He was educated in his father's library and at Oxford. (The latter university and Cambridge contend over the ancientness of their founding. Gibbon was to write, much later, that the only certain thing is that both of the venerable institutions exhibited all the infirmities and symptoms of the most advanced decrepitude.) At the age of sixteen the reading of Bossuet converted him to Catholicism. His alarmed family sent him to Lausanne, the center of Protestant orthodoxy. The unforeseen result of this maneuver was that Gibbon became a skeptic. Like Milton he always knew himself to be predestined to literature. He planned a history of the Swiss Confederation, but the difficulty of studying an obscure German dialect deterred him. He also thought of writing a biography of Sir Walter Raleigh, a theme that he sidestepped because he thought that such a book would have only local interest. In 1764 he went to Rome, and among the ruins of the Capital he conceived the plan of his most vast work, *The Decline and Fall of the Roman Empire*. Before writing a line he read in the original languages all the ancient and medieval historians and studied monuments and numismatics. He devoted eleven years to this labor, which ended in Lausanne on June 27, 1787. Seven years later he died in London.

Two qualities which seem mutually exclusive, irony and pomposity, come together in Gibbon's work, which is the most important historical monument in English literature, and one of the most important in the world. Gibbon chose a title that left him the greatest amplitude. His history covers thirteen centuries, from Trajan to the fall of Constantinople and the tragic fate of Rienzi. He was a master of the art of narration. The most diverse persons and events pass vividly through his pages: Charlemagne, Attila, Mahomet, Tamerlane, the sack of Rome, the Crusades, the spread of Islam, the eastern wars, and

those of the Germanic nations. He abounds in biting ob-
servations. The Scots boasted of being the only European
nation that had turned back the Romans. Gibbon observes
that the masters of the world turned their backs with disdain on that harsh, cloudy, and glacial land. There were
"nightly battles of theology" which in the same paragraph
he dubs "that ecclesiastical labyrinth." Nietzsche was to
write that Christianity was, at its origin, a religion of
slaves; Gibbon prefers to praise the mysterious decisions
of God, who commended the revelation of Truth not to
grave and learned philosophers, but to a small group of
illiterates. He does not deny the miracles, but censures the
unpardonable negligence of the pagan observers who,
while noting all the prodigious happenings of the world,
had said not a word about the resurrection of Lazarus or
the earthquake and the eclipse of the sun on the day of
the crucifixion of Jesus. From the time of Tacitus, many
persons had pondered the pious fervor of the Germans,
who did not enclose their gods in temples but preferred
to worship them in the depths of the forests. Gibbon's
comment is that people who were barely capable of con-
structing a hut could hardly be expected to build temples.[22]

Before writing in English, he wrote in French and in
Latin. This discipline, to which he joined a study of Pascal
and Voltaire, prepared him for the execution of his great
work. Its publication brought him bitter polemics of a
theological character which amused him a great deal, and
which he always won. To *The Decline and Fall of the
Roman Empire* we may add his treatise on the mysteries
of Eleusis and an admirable autobiography which was
published after his death.

Another illustrious writer of the eighteenth century

Boswell, who was of noble origin, was born in Edinburgh, at whose university he studied law, as he did at Glasgow and at Utrecht. The capital event of his life was his encounter with "Dictionary Johnson" in a bookstore in London. On the continent he became acquainted with Rousseau, Voltaire, and General Paoli of Corsica. He wrote an ode in favor of slavery, reasoning that its abolition would close for humanity the door to mercy, since the negroes in Africa would thereby be induced to kill their prisoners instead of selling them to the whites. In 1769 Boswell married Margaret Montgomery, his cousin, by whom he had seven children. A short time ago his manuscript diaries were discovered.[25] They were published in 1950 and abound in curious indiscretions of a personal nature.

[6]

The Romantic Movement

Oswald Spengler, the famous philosopher of history, includes in a brief list of the great Romantic poets the almost forgotten name of James MacPherson (1736–1796). He was born near Inverness in a region where the Gaelic language was still spoken. MacPherson himself never spoke it fluently nor learned to read it, but he felt a deep sense of pride in being Scottish. He was a schoolmaster. In 1760 with the aid of a friend, he published *Fragments of Ancient Poetry Collected in the Highlands of Scotland and Translated from the Gallic or Erse Language,* which was greeted with enthusiasm. Two years later, under the patronage of Dr. Blair, a distinguished man of letters, he published the epic *Fingal,* translated, the prologue explains, from a third-century poem preserved in the mountains and islands of Scotland, and whose author, Ossian, was the son of Fingal, the hero. This work, which was written in a rhythmical prose that recalls the verses of the Bible, was translated into nearly all the languages of Europe. One of its many readers was Napoleon, who carried a copy of the Italian version by Abbé Cesarotti with him during his campaign. Another reader was Goethe, who declared that Ossian had displaced Homer in his heart and who included a passage from it in his *Werther*. Others, nevertheless, affirmed that *Fingal* was apocryphal. The most violent against it was Dr. Johnson, who detested the Scots. He even said that it was absurd to attribute a poem in six books to a tribe of barbarians incapable of counting up to five. *Fingal* is perhaps not an authentic reconstruction of a Celtic epic, but it is beyond cavil the first romantic poem in European literature.[26] MacPherson was a poet who deliberately sacrificed himself for the greater glory of Scotland.

We transcribe: "Chief mixes his strokes with chief, and man with man: steel, clanging, sounds on steel. Helmets are cleft on high. Blood bursts and smokes around. Strings murmur on the polished yews. Darts rush along the sky. Spears fall like the circles of light, which gild the face of night: as the noise of the troubled ocean, when roll the waves on high." In another place he says: "My soul is full of other times." In another: "They saw battle in his face; the death of armies on his spear. A thousand shields at once are placed on their arms; they drew a thousand swords."

Outside Great Britain Lord Byron continues to be the central figure of English romanticism. Nowadays in his own country his work is less alive than his image. Handsome, sombre, and libertine, this aristocrat traveled through Spain, Portugal, Greece, Turkey, Germany, Switzerland, and Italy amidst an atmosphere of mystery and scandal. Lame from birth, he overcame the defect and swam the Dardanelles like the mythological Leander. Desiring to participate in the Greek war of independence, he nevertheless died of fever at Missolonghi on April 19,

1824. He was thirty-six years old. To the Greeks he is still a national hero.

Of his vast work we shall mention *Childe Harold,* a poem fantastic and autobiographical at the same time and whose next to last canto describes the battle of Waterloo. *Don Juan* is a sort of satirical epic which abounds in unforeseen episodes and erotic scenes. Byron rimed with extraordinary facility. In *Don Juan* he was prodigal of burlesque rimes of the sort that Leopoldo Lugones was to use in his *Lunario sentimental.*[27]

Officially the romantic movement begins in 1798, the year in which the *Lyrical Ballads* of Wordsworth and Coleridge appeared. Both are great poets; both are virtually untranslatable. The poetic theory of Wordsworth is interesting as well as learned. He explained it two years later in the *Preface* to the second edition of the *Ballads.* According to him, poetry is not the product of the moment when one experiences an emotion, but when the poet relives it and is at once actor and spectator: "Poetry is the spontaneous overflow of powerful feelings; it takes its origin from emotion recollected in tranquility." Wordsworth also rebels against the so-called poetic diction of the eighteenth century and against conventions and allegories. He required an immediate language, although he forbade the use of dialectal forms.[28] In his opinion city men had a more artificial way of speech than country dwellers, who are influenced by nature. Thus he prepares the way for Walt Whitman and Kipling, who would doubtless have scandalized him. But no one can manage to be entirely different from his times, and Wordsworth is sometimes guilty of the defects that he censures. He was born near the Scottish border in 1770 and died in 1850.

He left unfinished a long philosophical poem including a dream whose protagonist is an Arab whose mission was to save from the second flood two fundamental works of humanity,[29] art and science. They are represented by a stone, which also stands for Euclid's geometry, and by a snail, representing all the poetry of the world. Wordsworth also cultivated the sonnet, of which he has left examples not inferior to those of Shakespeare and Keats. Chesterton said that reading Wordsworth is like drinking a cup of water in the mountains at dawn.

Of Samuel Taylor Coleridge (1772–1834) it can almost be said that he has no biography. He was born in Devonshire, the son of a Protestant minister who delighted his rustic parishioners by inserting in his sermons long passages "in the very language of the Holy Spirit," that is to say, in Hebrew. Like Wordsworth, Coleridge favored the French Revolution and planned the founding of a socialist colony in the wilds of America. The reign of terror and the military dictatorship of Napoleon led him away from these ideas. His whole life consisted of a long series of postponements and distractions, of monumental works, of which mere indications remain, and of lectures announced and seldom delivered. He did conclude a prose work entitled *Biographia Literaria,* which contains, among an infinite number of digressions, a refutation of Wordsworth's theories, and some plagiarisms, conscious or not, of Fichte and Schelling. Together with De Quincey and Carlyle, he was one of the first popularizers in England of German philosophy. His poetical works consist of some four hundred pages, but except for "Dejection: An Ode," they may be reduced to three poems which some have said form a sort of *Divine Comedy.* The first, "Christabel," would correspond to hell; and the second, "The Rime of the Ancient Mariner," to purgatory. Its story is one of mysterious expiation; its locale is the antarctic regions, described with extraordinary vividness; the characters are men, angels, and demons. The third poem, "Kubla Khan," would represent paradise. Its development is curious. Coleridge, who was an opium-eater, had been reading a book of travels, and he dreamed a triple dream of a musical, verbal, and visual nature. He heard a voice repeating a poem, heard strange music, saw the construction of a Chinese palace, and he knew (as in dreams one knows such things) that the music was building the palace and that it belonged to Kubla Khan, the emperor who protected Marco Polo. The poem was meant to be quite long. Coleridge remembered his dream on awakening and began to write it down, but he was interrupted and could never remember the conclusion. The fifty-odd verses that he salvaged are, for their imagery and delicate cadence, one of the immortal pages of literature. Years after the death of the poet it was discovered that the emperor had built his palace according to a plan that had been revealed to him in a dream.

Thomas De Quincey (1785-1859) was a disciple of Coleridge and Wordsworth. Except for the novel *Klosterheim, or, The Masque,* and a translation or paraphrase of Lessing's *Laokoon,* his entire work, which fills fourteen volumes, is made up of articles, which in those days were the equivalent, in breadth and profundity, to what we should call books. Like Sir Thomas Browne he tried and frequently succeeded in writing a prose as poetic as verse. The *Confessions of an English Opium-Eater* (partly translated into French by Baudelaire) is his most important work. It tells of his bizarre exploits, his visions, and his nightmares. He sought an intellectual pleasure in opium. It increased his sensitivity to music and allowed him to understand, or believe that he understood, the most abstruse pages of Kant. He reached the point of taking eight to twelve thousand drops of laudanum a day. As the years passed, his nightmares oppressed him. Space was expanded to a degree that the human eye could not take in. A single night lasted centuries and he awakened worn out. Visions of the Orient pursued him; in sleep he thought himself the idol and the pyramid. His delicate and intricate paragraphs open like cathedrals of music. Small, fragile, and strangely urbane, his image lives on in the memory of men like a character in fiction, rather than a reality.

We have barely room to mention the names of the poet Shelley (1792–1822) or Sir Walter Scott (1771–1832), who begins the historical novel.

The most lofty of English lyric poets, John Keats (1795–1821), was born in London of humble parents and died of tuberculosis in Italy. His education was fragmentary: Arnold said of him that without a knowledge of Greek he was a born Greek. At twenty he wrote the famous sonnet "On First Looking into Chapman's Homer," in which he compares his amazement to that of the first Spanish conqueror who saw the Pacific. He was the friend of Leigh Hunt and Shelley. Milton had wanted poetry to be simple, sensual, and passionate. Keats's work, aside from his archaisms, fulfills this doctrine splendidly. Two of his poems, "Ode to a Nightingale" and "Ode on a Grecian Urn," will last as long as the English language. Keats made arrangements for the epitaph "Here lies one whose name was writ in water" to be engraved on his tomb. Shelley lamented his death in the famous elegy, "Adonais."

[7]

The Nineteenth Century
ᓚ Prose

At the beginning of the nineteenth century, the Protestant faith, the Romantic revolt against French classicism, the Napoleonic wars, the shared victory of Waterloo in which the Prussians and the English were brothers in arms, plus the memory of a common origin, brought England and Germany together. In literature the most emphatic representative of this rapprochement was Thomas Carlyle (1795–1881), the essayist and historian. In 1836 under the influence of John Paul Richter's style, he published the eloquent mystification *Sartor Resartus* (i.e., the *Tailor Retailored*).[30] This book relates the biography, expounds the doctrine, and contains long passages from the work of an imaginary, idealistic philosopher, Diogenes Teufelsdroeckh. Carlyle thought of universal history as a sort of divine cryptography which we are reading and writing continuously "and in which we are also written down." He thought that democracy was nothing more than a chaos provided by the voting booth, and so he put his faith in the principle of authority. He venerated Cromwell, Frederick the Great, Bismarck, William the Conqueror, and Dr. Francia, the dictator of Paraguay. During the war of the secession (U.S.A.), he was on the side of slavery. He declared that it seemed to him more convenient to have slaves one's whole life long than to change them occasionally. He affirmed that the state of England was deplorable, but that every town contained two things that cheered him: a military garrison and a jail. In these at least there was order. Among his principal works we may cite *On Heroes, Hero Worship, and the Heroic in History; The French Revolution, a History; Oliver Cromwell's Letters and Speeches; Past and Present;* and a history of *The Early Kings of Norway,* which sums up enthusiastically the classic work of the Icelander Snorri Sturluson. He believed in the superiority of the Nordic races, and with Fichte was one of the forerunners of Nazism. In his private life he was an unhappy and neurotic man.

Aside from a few biographical details the only certain thing that can be said of Charles Dickens (1812–1870) is that he was a man of genius. Stevenson was to accuse him of "plunging naked into the sentimental," but we must not forget that he cultivated not only the sentimental but also the humorous, the grotesque, the supernatural, and the tragic. Like his French contemporary Victor Hugo, he was a great romantic novelist. He bequeathed to the world a gallery of characters which, though often little more than caricatures, are also imperishable. The son of a poor office worker who was more than once jailed for debt and who in the novel *David Copperfield* is called Mr. Micawber, Dickens was no stranger to poverty. As a child he worked in a warehouse; he was a reporter of parliamentary sessions, a newspaper man, a magazine editor, and a novelist who published his books in installments. He traveled around the United States where he argued, to the scandal of his hearers, for the rights of authors and the abolition of slavery. Byron, Scott, and Wordsworth had discovered the beauty of the sea and the mountains; Dickens discovered the emotions of the slums. Another and even more important discovery of his was the solitary magic of childhood. The theme of crime also attracted him; and the murders he relates, which influenced Dostoevski, are unforgettable. Let us recall, among the many possible examples, the death of Montague Trigg at the hands of Jonas Chuzzlewit, which, although it is indirectly described, is nonetheless memorable. Dickens died prosperous. He left an unfinished detective novel, *The Mystery of Edwin Drood,* of which Chesterton remarked that the enigma will only be revealed when we meet Dickens in heaven, and then it will be most probable that he will not remember it. Dickens's father had a copy of *The Thousand and One Nights* and one of *Don Quixote.* It is probable that the latter, in which the open road is the source of adventures, so to speak, had an influence on *The Posthumous Papers of the Pickwick Club,* the book that made Dickens famous.

In addition to being a creator of characters Dickens was what we would call today an *engagé,* and a partisan of the outcasts. He advocated school and prison reform.

Dickens was led to the detective genre by the example of his intimate friend William Wilkie Collins (1824–1889). The latter wrote, among other works, *The Moonstone, The Woman in White,* and *Armadale.* T. S. Eliot thought that the first-named is not only the longest but the best of all the detective novels ever written. Under the influence of the epistolary novel of the eighteenth century, Collins was the first novelist to have the story told by one of the characters in the novel. This idea of supplying various points of view was used and expanded later by Robert Browning and Henry James.

In Thomas Babington Macaulay (1800–1859) come together, as in the person of Menéndez y Pelayo, a great writer and an uncommon intelligence. Both had the benefit of a prodigious memory. Both leave us the impression of having read all the books. Here the similarities end. Menéndez y Pelayo was a fervent Catholic, Macaulay a lukewarm and liberal Protestant. Another difference is to be found in their imagination: Macaulay was able to evoke intrigues and battles in a vivid manner.[31]

The son of Zachary Macaulay, a well-known abolitionist, Thomas inherited his father's ideas, which coincided with those of his times. From an early age he knew that he would be a historian. He understood that writing history required the previous study of books and archives. His economic circumstances were modest, and so he accepted a legal post in India, where he lived for five years saving money. On his return to England, he undertook after laborious research a brilliant though not impartial history of England, which he was to leave unfinished. He was also an admirable essayist. Among the many others, the articles we recall are those dedicated to Samuel Johnson, Clive, the creator of the British power in India, Joseph Addison, Milton, Petrarch, and Dante. He observed that the concrete details of the last named show more imagination than all the splendid vagaries of Milton. His attempts to write poetry achieved a popular success. He thought that, in addition to their Horace and their Virgil, the Romans must have had their romances and their ballads; and inspired by this idea, he wrote the *Lays of Ancient Rome,* which are still widely read in all countries where English is spoken. In the *Lays* he demonstrated, or at least implied, as Kipling did later, the fundamental identity of all empires.

In contrast to Macauley, John Ruskin (1819–1900) was a very complex man. Painting, of which he was a practiced devotee, interested him as did architecture, social problems, and the art of prose. He is regarded as a preeminent English stylist. In his last years he gave up the delicate cadences which so delighted Wilde and Proust and reduced himself, aesthetically, to a bare and almost puerile prose. Since he was a wealthy man, he regarded his fortune as part of the public patrimony, and each year he published in *The Times* a minute rendering of his accounts so that people might see that he had not wasted his income to the detriment of everyone else. He founded a school for workmen. His most extensive work is *Modern Painters.* The first volume appeared in 1843, the fifth and last in 1860. This work, which abounds in curious digressions, was begun in defense of Turner, whom he considered the world's greatest landscape painter. Among his other books, almost all of them polemic in character, are *The Seven Lamps of Architecture, The Stones of Venice, Elements of Drawing, Elements of Perspective, The Political Economy of Art, The Ethics of the Dust, Sesame and Lilies, The Eagle's Nest,* and *Praeterita.* He was a patron of the Pre-Raphaelite painters and poets, of whom more will be said later on.

Ruskin denied to the ancients and the Middle Ages a sentiment of nature. He said that for Homer a beautiful place was a fertile place and that the mountains and forests so much appreciated by the romantics terrified Dante. He thought that pictures ought to be painted in semicircular form, since this would correspond to our vision. He thought that the habit of rectangular form was based on the maleficent influence of walls, doors, and windows. He opposed the construction of railway stations because no verse in the Bible speaks of iron buildings. He accused the American painter Whistler of cheating.

The work of Matthew Arnold (1822–1888) was also complex. The nature of this outline precludes a consideration of the political and theological controversies to which he devoted a part of his life. He was born in the county of Middlesex and educated at Rugby and Oxford, to which he always remained faithful. He was an inspector of schools and held the Oxford chair of poetry. Renan, Sainte-Beuve, and Wordsworth were his favorite authors. Under Carlyle's influence, England in those years considered herself purely Germanic, but in a famous essay, *On the Study of Celtic Literature,* Arnold declared that the Celtic element was no less important, and he recalled the melancholy of MacPherson, which had captivated all Europe, and cited passages from Shakespeare and Byron which, according to him, had nothing Saxon about them. He thought that arbitrariness was the besetting sin of English writers. He sought "sweetness and light" in the study of the French, the Greeks, and the Romans. He admired Goethe and accused Carlyle, who was presumed to be his disciple, of never having understood him. More than once he denounced the provincialism of his country.

He wrote articles on Heine and Maurice de Guérin. He toured the United States giving a series of lectures, but the new world did not arouse him to much enthusiasm. The most famous of his works, *On Translating Homer,* argues that literal translation is usually unfaithful since it creates emphases and effects which do not correspond to the original and which detain and surprise the reader as they should not do. Thus when Captain Burton gave his translation the title *The Thousand and One Nights,* he was proposing, according to Arnold, a translation which does not correspond to the Arabic, since in that language the phrase "a thousand nights and one night" is habitual. His poetry, which is less important than his prose,[32] has been judged severely by T. S. Eliot. Arnold had a positive influence on his generation; his distinction, his irony and urbanity are beyond dispute. Stevenson declared that of all the qualities of a writer, one alone is of value: charm, and no one can deny that Arnold possessed it.

The Reverend Charles Lutwidge Dodgson (1832–1898) was what Arnold never was and would never have wished to be, an eccentric Englishman. As he was singularly shy, he fled from dealings with adults and sought the friendship of children. To amuse a little girl named Alice Liddell,[33] he wrote under the pseudonym Lewis Carroll the two books that were to make him famous, *Alice's Adventures in Wonderland* and *Through the Looking-Glass.* In the first Alice dreams that she is pursuing a white rabbit. The chase leads her through the woods to a land of fantastic beings, among whom are kings and queens from a deck of cards, who judge and condemn until she discovers that they are only playing cards and

[8]

The Nineteenth Century
~ Poetry

The poet, painter, and engraver William Blake (1757–1827) is, like William Langland, one of the great mystics of England. Chronologically he was the contemporary of the romantics. Mentally he was a neoplatonist, like Swedenborg and Nietzsche.[37] Swedenborg had said that man's redemption should be not only moral but intellectual. Blake confirms this: "The fool will not enter paradise, however saintly he be." He adds that redemption must also be aesthetic, for thus Jesus Christ understood it, teaching his doctrine in parables, that is to say, in poems. He prefers vengeance to pardon, reasoning that every injured person wants to avenge himself, and if he does not, the unsatisfied desire—and this anticipates Freud—will sicken his soul. A half-century later, Ruskin will recommend to painters the patient observation of nature; Blake declares that such an exercise annuls and dulls the artist's imagination. He wrote that the doors of perception, that is, the five senses, hide the universe from us and if we could

48

block them off we would see it as it is, infinite and eternal. In *The Marriage of Heaven and Hell,* which has been translated into Spanish by Pablo Neruda,[38] he inquires whether a bird which "cuts the airy way" is not perhaps "a world of delight, clos'd by your senses five." He created a personal mythology whose divinities were called Los and Enitharmon, Oothoon and Urizen. The problem of evil tormented him. The best known of his poems asks upon what anvil and in what forge God, who made the lamb, made the tiger "burning bright, in the forests of the night." In another poem he speaks to us of "a region of interwoven labyrinths." In another a goddess arms herself with nets of iron and snares of diamonds and hunts for her love "girls of smooth silver and furious gold."

In 1789 he published in regular verse his *Songs of Innocence;* in 1794, *Songs of Innocence and of Experience.* Later appeared the long series of his *Prophetic Books,* composed in rhythmic verse paragraphs that anticipate Walt Whitman and contain a complicated mythology. As a painter and engraver of the eighteenth century, he already anticipates the expressionists. He died still singing.

Two great poets dominate the heterogeneous and turbulent era which we have agreed to call Victorian and which today we characterize as unruffled: Tennyson and Browning. It is impossible to conceive of two more different personalities and impossible to imagine a firmer friendship.

Alfred Tennyson (1809-1892) was the son of a Protestant minister. He was educated in a literary atmosphere; his father and brothers were poets. He was an alumnus of Trinity College, Cambridge. Contemporary problems worried him: he tried to reconcile the first chapter of Genesis with recent geological discoveries, the theory of the evolution, the conflicts and aspirations of democracy, and the future of humanity; but, as in the case of other great poets, the essential part of his work is to be found in the music of his verse. An admirable line such as "Far on the ringing plains of windy Troy." [39] is quite evidently untranslatable. Helen speaks, raises her eyes, and the poet does not know when she has become silent. She has covered the interval of sound with light. In another poem, after a night of orgy the libertines come out into the street and look at the sky. God has made with the dawn a "terrible rose." Tennyson's most important work is his long philosophical elegy "In Memoriam," which describes the various states of the soul of a man in despair over the death of someone he loves. In 1850 he accepted the title of Poet Laureate. He admired no writer so much as Virgil.

In contrast to Tennyson, Robert Browning (1812–1889) sought music in harshness rather than in sweetness in the manner of his Saxon antecedents. Individuals interested him more than abstract problems. He specialized in dramatic monologues, using persons real or imaginary; for instance, Napoleon III and Caliban come face to face and justify themselves. His work is enigmatic. During his lifetime a society was founded to analyze it. Browning attended the meetings, cheered each interpreter on, and then abstained from all intervention. He lived a great deal in Italy and was passionately devoted to its liberation. In the poem "How It Strikes a Contemporary," which is laid in Valladolid, Spain, the protagonist may be Cervantes, a mysterious spy of God, or the Platonic archetype of a poet. In his "An Epistle, Containing the Strange Medical Experience of Karshish, the Arab Physician," an Arab doctor describes the resurrection of Lazarus and the odd indifference he displayed in later life as if it were a clinical case. In "My Last Duchess," an Italian aristocrat permits us to guess, without any show of remorse, that he has poisoned his wife. His chief work is *The Ring and the Book*. Ten different persons, among them the protagonists, the assassin, the persons assassinated, the presumed lover, the prosecutor for the crown, the defense attorney, and the pope, relate in detail the story of a crime. The facts are identical, but each character believes that his actions have been just. If Browning had not chosen to write in verse he would have been a great storyteller, not inferior to Conrad or Henry James.

Of Edward Fitzgerald (1809–1883) it might be said that he was a great minor poet. He was educated at Cambridge and lived a retired, idle, and modest life with no other task than to work everlastingly at his verse and correspond with friends. His talent required an outside stimulus, the less accessible the better. He translated without special felicity the dramas of Calderon and Euripides. In 1859 he published anonymously the brief work which was to give him imperishable fame: the *Rubaiyat of Omar Khayyam*. Omar Khayyam was a distinguished Persian astronomer of the eleventh century, who left on the periphery of his mathematical studies some one hundred disconnected stanzas, rimed *a a b a*. Of these Fitzgerald made a poem, translating them freely and beginning with the stanzas that refer to morning, springtime, and wine, and ending with those that speak of night, desperation, and death.

The son of Italian parents, whose revolutionary activities led them to take refuge in England, Dante Gabriel Rossetti (1828–1882) was born in London, where he spent almost all his life. Painter and poet he founded in 1848 the Pre-Raphaelite Brotherhood,[40] whose fundamental doctrine was that the painter Raphael signified not the height but the decadence of painting. This doctrine, which led him to the study and imitation of the primitives, exceeds the limits of this book. He was married in 1860. Two years later his wife committed suicide. Rossetti, who had been unfaithful to her, thought himself responsible and therefore placed on the dead woman's breast the manuscript of a book which he was to exhume eight years later and which would make him famous.[41] Neuroses, insomnia, the overuse of chloral, and voluntary solitude marked the end of his life.

Throughout the work of Rossetti one breathes an atmosphere of the hothouse and of sickly beauty. The most famous of his poems, "The Blessed Damozel," is the story of a girl in heaven who, as she leans over the golden parapet, is waiting and will always wait for the arrival of her lover. The revelation is gradual; paradise borders on nightmare. No less admirable are his narrative poems "Eden Bower" and "Troy Town." Of the series of sonnets that form "The House of Life" we shall mention one that concerns the battle of Waterloo. The poet thinks of the thousands of men whose dust is there and asks himself whether there is a single place on earth that is not soaked with human blood.

An intimate friend of the unfortunate Rossetti, William Morris (1834–1896) was an indefatigable, energetic, and probably happy man. He is considered one of the fathers of English socialism. A disciple of John Ruskin, he became the master of George Bernard Shaw. He revived interest in the arts of decoration, furniture, and typography. In 1858 he published *The Defense of Guenevere, and Other Poems,* which is full of vague, medieval music. One composition is entitled "Two Red Roses across the Moon," another, "The Tune of Seven Towers." Nine years later appeared *The Life and Death of Jason,* a long, ponderous epic which relates, with a coupling together of circumstantial inventions and fine pathetic traits, the undertaking of the Argonauts and the love of Medea. His greatest work, *The Earthly Paradise,* belongs to the years 1868–1870. As in the *Canterbury Tales* one story serves as a framework for the rest. In the fourteenth century a group of Norwegians and Bretons, fleeing from the plague, sailed in search of the Fortunate Isles, where they hoped to find immortality. They did not reach their goal, but after laborious navigation they arrived old and despairing at a western island where Greek was still spoken. Each month they met with the elders of the city to exchange stories. Of the twenty-four tales, twelve are classical, the other twelve Scandinavian, Celtic, or Arabic. In 1871 Morris managed his first journey, almost a pilgrimage, to Iceland, which he regarded as a sacred land. He conceived the plan, perhaps unrealizable, of using a purely Germanic English. In this fashion he translated the first verses of the *Odyssey:*

Tell me, o Muse, of the Shifty, the man who wandered afar,
After the Holy Burg, Troy-town, he had wasted with war, . . .

which suggests less the Mediterranean than the seas of the north.

53

He translated the *Aeneid* and *Beowulf*. The Scottish humanist Andrew Lang said that the language of this last version was somewhat more archaic than the original, which dates from the eighth century. Of Morris's other works the most extensive and ambitious is the epic *The Story of Sigurd, the Volsung,* whose theme is the same as that of the *Nibelungenlied*. Morris also published a useful library of sagas.[42] Despite the ponderousness for which some critics reproach him, he was a great poet.

The great erotic poet Charles Algernon Swinburne (1837–1909) also belonged to the circle of Morris and Rossetti. He brought to the English language a new music. His poetry, even more than that of Tennyson, is untranslatable. Let us recall, however, the poem "Laus Veneris," whose protagonist is Tannhäuser, who does not repent of his sin, as well as a fine elegy dedicated to Baudelaire.[43]

[9]

The End of the
Nineteenth Century

The brief courageous life of the Scotsman Robert Louis
Stevenson (1850–1894) was a struggle against tuberculosis
which pursued him from Edinburgh to London, from
London to the south of France, from France to California, and from California to an island in the Pacific,
where it finally caught up with him. Despite this handi-
cap, or perhaps urged on by it, he left important work
which contains no single careless page but does indeed
have many splendid ones. One of his first books, the
New Arabian Nights, anticipates the vision of a fantastic
London which was rediscovered much later by his fervent
biographer Gilbert Chesterton. This series includes the
story of *The Suicide Club.* In 1886 he published *The
Strange Case of Dr. Jekyll and Mr. Hyde.* It should be
observed that this brief novel was read as if it were a
detective story, and the revelation that the two protagonists were one and the same must come as a surprise.
The scene of the transformation was revealed to Steven-

son in a dream. The theory and practice of style always preoccupied him. He wrote that a verse consists in satisfying an expectation in a direct form, while prose is the art of resolving it in an unexpectedly pleasant way. His essays and short stories are excellent. Among the first we cite *Pulvis et umbra,* among the second *Markheim,*[44] which tells the story of a crime. Of his extraordinary novels we shall only recall *The Master of Ballantrae,* whose theme is the hatred of two brothers, and the *Wier of Hermiston* which is unfinished. In his poetry he alternates between literary English and the Scottish dialect. As in the case of Kipling the fact of his having written for children has perhaps diminished his fame. *Treasure Island* has caused the essayist, novelist, and poet to be forgotten.[45] Stevenson is one of the most lovable and heroic figures in English literature.

The scandalous story of the lawsuit, imprudently undertaken by Oscar Wilde (1854–1900) against the Marquess of Queensberry, whom he accused of defamation, has contributed in paradoxical fashion to give him notoriety and to tarnish the innocence and lightheartedness of his work. Wilde recommended an aestheticism without too much believing in it. He preached the doctrine of art for art's sake with a smile and said that there are no moral or immoral books, just well-written or badly written ones. His first comedies suffer somewhat from sentimental excesses; his last, *The Importance of Being Earnest,* or as Alfonso Reyes translates it *La Importancia de ser Severo* (*The Importance of Being Stern*), is a delightful and purely simple game of absurdities. Wilde was a brilliant conversationalist. His friends relate that the oral version of his short stories was generally better than the written one, since in the latter he over-loaded them with jewelry, silks, and precious metals. Of his poems we shall mention "The Sphinx" and "The Harlot's House," which are above all decorative pieces.[46] His only novel, *The Picture of Dorian Gray,* is, as it were, overburdened with epigrams and excessive preciosity. Of another sort is the pathetic *The Ballad of Reading Gaol,* written after two years of forced labor. His aesthetic essays are admirable. Of his verbal cleverness we cite two examples: "One of those characteristic British faces that, once seen, are never remembered" and "Oh, my dear friend, only a deaf man could wear a tie like yours with impunity."

Storyteller, novelist, and poet Rudyard Kipling (1865–1936) took upon himself the task of revealing to his indifferent fellow countrymen the existence of the far-flung British empire. Many blamed him for this mission, and still do for his political opinions, but not for the remarkable genius of his literary work. He was born in Bombay and died in England. One might say that he went from geography to history, from space to time. He felt in Europe what he had hardly felt at all in Asia, the pull of the past. He was a master of the short story, from his first narratives, which were simple and brief, up to the last ones which were no less complex and agonizing than those of Henry James. The novel *Kim* leaves the impression that we have known all India and have spoken to thousands of persons. The two protagonists, the Buddhist monk and the street boy, each seek their own salvation; the one through the meditative life; the other through action. This very precise and lively novel is, as it were, saturated with magic. The importance of Kipling's poetry, which is looked down upon somewhat by contemporary critics who could not forgive him his popularity, has been recognized by T. S. Eliot. In a time of lavish and melancholy poetry Kipling burst upon the literary world with his *Barrack-Room Ballads,*[47] written in popular jargon. He was always in search of the epic. Among his last poems we may mention "The Harp Song of the Dead Women" and "The Runic Characters on the Sword of Weland."

He had a strange literary fate. Copies of his books, translated into many languages, were sold by the thousands. The Swedish Academy conferred the Nobel prize on him. Meanwhile Kipling lived in the solitude of his Burwash house, overwhelmed by the successive deaths of his children.

The first books of H. G. Wells (1866–1946) foretell and, as they are a half-century ahead of their time, undoubtedly surpass the works now called science fiction. As he was poor and ill, Wells transmuted his bitterness into those unforgettable and splendid nightmares: *The Time Machine, The Invisible Man, The First Men in the Moon, The Country of the Blind* (short stories), and *The Island of Dr. Moreau.* His other novels correspond to the Dickens tradition: *Kipps, The Wheels of Chance,* and the satiric *Tono-Bungay.* Wells, like George Bernard Shaw, belonged to the Fabian Society. His curious book *The Open Conspiracy* declares that the present division of the planet into different countries, ruled by different governments, is entirely arbitrary, and that men of goodwill will end by coming together to dispense with the present forms of the state. Nations and governments will disappear, not by revolution but because people will understand that they are totally artificial. Wells was one of the founders of the Pen Club whose purpose was to promote a union of the world's writers. In the last years of his life he voluntarily gave up his fantasies and compiled for the instruction of humanity works of an encyclopedic nature.[48] One is reminded of the analogous case of Ruskin, who renounced his splendid style for the public benefit. In 1934 Wells wrote his *Experiment in Autobiography* in which he tells of his humble origins, his wretched adolescence, his scientific training, his two marriages, and his varied and turbulent sentimental life. Hilaire Belloc accused him of being a provincial Englishman. Wells replied: "Mr. Belloc, it seems, was born all over Europe." Anatole France said of him that he was "the greatest intellectual force in the English-speaking world."

The famous Irish dramatist George Bernard Shaw (1856-1950) discovered his dramatic vocation at the age of thirty-six. Before that he had been a critic of music and of theater.[49] He attacked Shakespeare and revealed to England the talents of Ibsen and Wagner. His first comedies have to do with tenements, prostitution, medicine, free love, the romantic concept of war, and the uselessness of vengeance. His last are openly fantastic and messianic, despite the humor that delights his readers. The nineteenth century had professed the Christian faith or believed in the survival of the fittest—that is to say, in a blind selection by fate. Shaw rejected both doctrines and preached the cult of energy in the manner of Blake, Schopenhauer, and Samuel Butler.[50] In *Man and Superman* he declares that heaven and hell are not places but conditions of the human soul; in *Back to Methuselah*, that a man should plan to live three hundred years in order not to die at eighty in his full immaturity, with a golf club in his hand; and that the material universe began with the spirit and will return to the spirit. This last doctrine coincides with that of the Irish theologian Scotus Erigena.[51] Shaw is one of the few writers of our time who has created heroic characters. One remembers Julius Caesar in *Caesar and Cleopatra,* Blanco Posnet, and Major Barbara, who says: "I have got rid of the bribe of heaven. Let God's work be done for its own sake: the work he had to create us to do because it cannot be done except by living men and women. When I die, let him be in my debt, not I in his; and let me forgive him as becomes a woman of my rank."

The prefaces of his dramatic works reveal him as an admirable and clear writer of prose, related to the best tradition of the eighteenth century. His peculiar sense of humor has drawn attention away from the essential seriousness of his work, which is among the most important of our time. In his dramas Shaw tries to justify the conduct and ethics of each character; even the inquisitors of Joan of Arc act, according to their own lights, in a reasonable manner.

In 1925 he won the Nobel Prize, accepting the honor but returning the money. Three years later his interest in the ways of mankind took him to Russia; in 1931, to India, Africa, China, and the United States. At ninety-four his indefatigable activity caused his death. While chopping down a tree in his yard at Bury St. Edmunds, he fell, fractured some bones, and died a few days later.

The Polish sea captain Jozef Teodor Konrad Naleçz Korzeniowski (1857–1924), famous as Joseph Conrad, is one of the greatest novelists and short story writers in the

English language. As in the case of George Bernard Shaw, his initiation to literature came late. His first book, *Almayer's Folly,* dates from 1895, when the author had already navigated the seven seas, gathering, without purposing to do so, experiences for his later work. He had decided to become a famous writer. He knew the limited geographical reach of his native tongue, and for a while he vacillated between French and English, which he handled with equal mastery.[52] He decided upon English, but he wrote with the sort of care and occasional formality which are proper to French prose. In 1898 he published *The Nigger of the Narcissus* and two years later *Lord Jim,* his masterpiece, the central theme of which is an obsession with honor and the shame of cowardice. In *Chance,* 1914, he employs a curious procedure. Two persons who have known a third person go about reconstructing, sometimes without any real certainty, the life of their acquaintance. Differing from his other novels, whose background is the sea, *The Secret Agent* describes in a singularly lively fashion the activities of a group of anarchists in London. Conrad, in a foreword, declares that he was never acquainted with an anarchist. His best stories are *Heart of Darkness, Youth, The Duel,* and *The Shadow-Line.* A critic maintained that the last named was of the fantastic sort. Conrad replied that to look for the fantastic was to show oneself insensible to the very nature of the world, which is always fantastic.

Sir Arthur Conan Doyle (1859–1930) was a writer of second rate to whom the world owes a single immortal character, Sherlock Holmes. This almost mythological being was constructed after the example of the gentleman detective Dupin created by Edgar Allan Poe, but he

that binds him to those who had wronged him. Another novel, *What Maisie Knew* (1897), hints at an atrocious story, seen through the innocent eyes of an ignorant young girl, who tells it without understanding it. His short stories are purposely ambiguous. The most discussed of all, *The Turn of the Screw,* admits of at least two interpretations. No one has been willing to concede that when James wrote it he was striving for all these different interpretations without identifying himself with any one. His last story, *The Sense of the Past* (1917), was never finished.[54] Under the influence of Wells's *Time Machine,* he relates the adventures of a young American who by dint of meditation and solitude returns to the eighteenth century and ends by discovering that just as he was a stranger in the present, he was one in the past as well. The life of Henry James must have been the same: reflecting isolation and a sense of exile. All men of letters acknowledged in him a master, but nobody reads his books. It is significant that in one of his stories, *The Great Good Place,* paradise appears under the guise of a luxurious sanatorium. He lived without hope, but he believed with all his heart in the importance and the subtlety of his work, which encompasses more than thirty volumes.

Gilbert Keith Chesterton (1874–1936) was not only the creator of Father Brown and an eloquent defender of the Catholic faith, but an essayist, an author of admirable biographies, a historian, and a poet as well. He studied drawing and painting and even illustrated some of his friend Hilaire Belloc's books. Then he devoted himself to literature, but there is in his writing a strong pictorial element. His characters come on the scene like actors, and his lively though unreal landscapes stick in our memory.

Chesterton lived through the melancholy years referred to as the *fin de siècle*. In a poem dedicated to Edmund Bentley, he declares, "The world was very old indeed when you and I were young." From this inescapable depression he was rescued by Whitman and Stevenson. Something of it stayed with him, however, and he retained a penchant for the horrible. The most famous of his novels, *The Man Who Was Thursday*, is subtitled *A Nightmare*. He could have been an Edgar Allan Poe or a Kafka; he preferred—and for this we are grateful—to be Chesterton. In 1911 he published an epic poem, *The Ballad of the White Horse*, which deals with the wars of Alfred the Great against the Danes. In it we encounter an extraordinary comparison: "Marble, like solid moonlight, gold like congealed fire." Another poem thus defines night: "A cloud larger than the world and a monster made of eyes." No less admirable is his *Ballad of Lepanto*. In the last stanza Captain Cervantes sheathes his sword and smiles as he thinks of a knight roaming the endless roads of Castille. The Father Brown stories are his most famous work. Each one suggests an impossible quandary which is then resolved in a rational manner.[55] During the eighteenth century paradox and wit had been used against religion. Chesterton used them in its defense. His apology for the Christian faith, *Orthodoxy* (1908), has been admirably turned into Spanish by Alfonso Reyes. In 1922 he moved from the Anglican church to Catholicism. Among his critical studies, we cite those devoted to Saint Francis, Saint Thomas, Chaucer, Blake, Dickens, Browning, Stevenson, and George Bernard Shaw. He also wrote a splendid universal history entitled *The Everlasting Man*. His total work exceeds a hundred volumes. Beneath his jokes was a profound erudition. His corpulence was famous: it is told of him that once on a bus he offered his seat to three ladies. Chesterton, the most popular writer of his time, is one of the most attractive figures in literature.

The son of a miner and a schoolteacher, David Herbert Lawrence (1885–1930) evoked his childhood in the novel *Sons and Lovers,* published in 1913. He became a primary school teacher, but his first novel, *The White Peacock* (1911), determined his vocation as a writer. A year later he settled in Italy with Frieda Weekley, and they were married in 1914. In the same year he published *The Prussian Officer.* After that came *The Rainbow, Twilight in Italy, The Lost Girl,* which won him a prize, *The Plumed Serpent,* and, after a trip to Australia, *Kangaroo.* He felt as did the pagans and Walt Whitman that there is something sacred about physical love. His three versions of *Lady Chatterley's Lover* try to express this conviction.[56] He does so at times in an explicit manner and at other times with extraordinary delicacy. This book, which kept him busy from 1925 to 1928, is perhaps his masterpiece; it is without doubt the most famous. Tuberculosis, which finally killed him, exacerbated his sensitivity and justifies his extreme positions.

The violence of Lawrence's detractors and defenders has possibly prejudiced his case. Today, now that these polemics have died down, we see in him a great writer.[57]

Thomas Edward Lawrence (1888–1935), called Lawrence of Arabia, is a legend, an epic personage, and the poetic author of the long prose epic *The Seven Pillars of Wisdom* (1926).[58] He studied at Oxford and was an archeologist. During the First World War he captained a rebellion of Arab tribes against the Turkish government.

His book has no other defect than to abound in intentionally anthological pages, describing that adventure. A man of extraordinary courage, Lawrence was at the same time very sensitive. In one instance he speaks of "the physical shame of victory." In another he praises the courage of an enemy regiment as follows: "For the first time in this campaign I was able to be proud of the courage of those who had killed my brothers." It was his opinion that in 1918 the Allies had betrayed the Arabs, and so he gave up all his honors—even his own name—and enlisted in the Air Force under the name of Shaw. He died in a motorcycle accident.

He was an excellent Hellenist. Among the thirty some versions of the *Odyssey* in English, his is one of the best.

Virginia Woolf (1882–1941) was educated in the library of her father, the well-known man of letters, Sir Leslie Stephen. Although hers was essentially a poetic nature, she nevertheless preferred the novel in which she attempted some curious experiments under the influence of Henry James and Proust.[59] Orlando, the hero of her most famous novel, of the same name,[60] is not only an individual, he is the archetype of an ancient family. He lives three hundred years and during his long story he changes sex. Other admirable novels of hers are: *Night and Day, Jacob's Room, Mrs. Dalloway, To the Lighthouse,* and *The Waves. Flush* tells the story of the Brownings as seen by their dog. In Virginia Woolf's books, plot is less important than changing states of consciousness and her delicate landscapes. Her style is at once visual and musical. She committed suicide by drowning herself in a river during the Second World War.

The Honorable Victoria Sackville-West (1892–1962)

belonged to the noble family that her friend Virginia Woolf personified in *Orlando*. In 1913 she married Harold Nicholson, a writer, British ambassador to Persia, and biographer of Verlaine and Swinburne. In 1927 she published the poem *The Land,* dedicated to the tasks and the days of the year, according to the seasons. Other poems of this georgic type are "The Garden," "Orchard and Vineyard," and "Some Flowers." Among the thirty volumes of her work three novels stand out: *The Edwardians, The Dark Island,* and *All Passions Spent,* whose title is taken from the last line of Milton's *Samson Agonistes.* In this story the telling is retrospective. An old woman, widow of a viceroy of India, is recalling her splendid past, but the weight of it all tells on her and she ends by freeing herself from it. This book, like *The Edwardians,* evokes with delicacy, irony, and not without poetry the feelings and habits of the English aristocracy at the beginning of the twentieth century. Miss West devoted a study to the first woman of letters who appeared in England, Mrs. Aphra Ben, a spy and the author of licentious works. She also wrote on the baroque poet Andrew Marvell, on Joan of Arc, and on Santa Teresa de Jesus.

The Irishman James Joyce (1882–1941) is, literally, one of the most extraordinary writers of our century. His greatest work, *Ulysses,* attempts to replace the unity that is lacking in his work with a system of labored and gratuitous symmetries. This novel, which is nine hundred pages long, chronicles the events of a single day. Each chapter corresponds to a color, to a function of the human body, to an organ, to a rhetorical procedure, and, with chronological precision, to a determined hour. Thus in one chapter the color red predominates, as does the circulation of the blood and use of hyperbole. In another, which is organized in the manner of a catechism, there are questions and answers. In still another, to express the protagonist's fatigue, the style becomes listless in parallel fashion and abounds in careless phrases and commonplaces. Furthermore, each episode corresponds, Stuart Gilbert has revealed,[61] to a book of the *Odyssey*. One chapter is hallucinatory in character and is made up of dialogues between ghosts and objects; it takes place in a house of ill repute in Dublin. Even more strange is *Finnegan's Wake,* which suggests the idea of an ending, of repetition, and of awakening. Just as *Ulysses* is a book of wakefulness, *Finnegan's Wake* is one of dreams. The hero is a Dublin tavern keeper, born in the city, and having in his veins Celtic, Scandinavian, Saxon, and Norman blood. While he dreams he becomes each of his forebears and every person in the world. The vocabulary of the novel, besides its prepositions and articles, consists mainly of compound words taken from various languages, including Icelandic and Sanskrit. After some years of labor two American scholars have published a book, unfortunately indispensable, entitled *A Skeleton Key to Finnegan's Wake.*[62]

The undeniable genius of Joyce was essentially verbal. It is a pity that he wasted it on the novel, instead of devoting it, as he but rarely did, to writing good poetry. The books that we have ennumerated are untranslatable; not so his stories called *The Dubliners* and the fine autobiographical novel *A Portrait of the Artist as a Young Man.*

During the First World War Joyce lived in Paris, Zurich, and Trieste. As he himself said, he worked in exile and longing. He died poor, tired, and blind in

Zurich. Virginia Woolf said of *Ulysses* that it is a glorious defeat.

William Butler Yeats (1865–1939) is, according to T. S. Eliot, the foremost poet of our time. His work is divided into two periods; the initial one belongs to what has been called the Celtic Twilight. It is characterized by the sweetness of its music; by its imagery, made deliberately vague; and by a frequent use of the ancient mythology of Ireland. During this period he was without doubt influenced by the Pre-Raphaelites.[63] His second period, which belongs to his maturity, reveals almost another man to us. The mythology that persists is no longer decorative or nostalgic, but pregnant with meaning. Furthermore, it alternates with lively and concrete, contemporary images. His verse seeks precision, not suggestion. Yeats believed in the existence of a universal memory, of which all individual memories are a part and which we may evoke through certain symbols. Theosophical speculation intrigued him, and like so many others he conceived a cyclical doctrine of history. This latter, according to his own declaration, was revealed to him by the spirit of an Arab traveler. The technique of Japanese dramatic art influenced his theatrical work, which was made purposely antirealistic. In one of his scenes the swords of warriors fall upon the shields of the enemy. Yeats indicates that the arms should not touch and that the sound of a gong should mark the imaginary clash.

The following verse, selected at random, is full of beauty and depth. A group of splendid women are coming slowly down a staircase. Someone asks why they were created, and this reply is given: "For desecration and the lover's night." Among Yeats's works we cite *The Land of Heart's Desire, The King's Threshhold, The Wind among the Reeds, In the Seven Woods, Per Amica Silentia Lunae, The Tower, The Winding Stair and Other Poems, Oedipus Rex,* and *Autobiographies.* In 1923 he was awarded the Nobel prize for literature.

The son of an engineer, Charles Langbridge Morgan (1894–1958) was born in the county of Kent. At the beginning of the First World War he was taken prisoner by the Germans and kept under parole for a period of four years in Holland. He used his knowledge of the country in his novel, *The Fountain.* Two of Morgan's essential themes are the spiritualization of human feelings and the conflict between love and duty. Three of his most important novels are *Portrait in a Mirror,* the story of a young man who is unable to finish the portrait of a beloved woman until he has fully understood her and until he knows that they will never meet again; *The Fountain,* which relates and analyzes the drama of two men and a woman who mutually love and respect each other; and *Sparkenbroke,* the most complex of all his books, which narrates the tormented desire for perfection and the final solitude of a writer. His style is slow moving because he is unwilling to be unfaithful to the beauty of the images and the delicate vicissitudes of emotion.

Like Henry James, Thomas Stearns Eliot (1888–1964) was born in the United States. He occupies in England and in the world a place analogous to that of Paul Valéry. He was at first a lucid and orderly disciple of the extravagant Ezra Pound. In 1922 he published his first famous poem, *The Wasteland;* twenty years later there appeared the curious volume of poems, *Four Quartets.* In one of these Eliot does not use words as a unit, for words are everyone's property, but uses unrelated verses, sometimes from another language. Thus, in successive lines he alternates a popular Australian music hall ballad with a line from Verlaine. In Argentina, Rafael Obligado has used the same artifice in the initial verse of his poem "Las Quintas de mi tiempo," but he sought a melancholy effect and not the striking contrast sought by Eliot. His plays, the characters of which are remembered with difficulty, have, above all, an experimental value. Eliot was in search of a verse form that would represent for our time what blank verse was to the age of Shakespeare. In *The Family Reunion* he revives the chorus, making it express what the characters feel but do not say. His critical work, which was studiously written, tends in general to exalt the neo-classicism of the eighteenth century at the expense of the Romantic movement. He included also studies on Dante, Milton, and the influence of Seneca on the Elizabethan theater.

In 1933 Eliot assumed British citizenship, and in 1948 he was awarded the Nobel prize. His verses will not allow us to forget the laborious erasures that occurred in writing them, but at times they are splendid and charged with nostalgia and solitude. Sometimes he achieves a Latin brevity. In one place he speaks to us of stags "which are engendered for the rifle." He wrote that in religion he was an Anglo-Catholic; in literature, a classicist; in politics, a partisan of monarchy.

Brief Bibliography

Chesterton, G. K. *The Victorian Age in Literature.*
Harvey, Sir Paul. *The Oxford Companion to English Literature.*
Kennedy, Charles W. *The Earliest English Poetry.*
Ker, W. P. *Medieval English Literature.*
Lang, Andrew. *History of English Literature.*
Legouis, Emile, and Cazamian, Louis. *A History of English Literature.*
Saintsbury, George. *A Short History of English Literature.*
Sampson, George. *The Concise Cambridge History of English Literature.*

Notes

¹ Kennings.

² E.g., the *Seafarer*.

³ In the *Exeter Book:* about 35 lines. The Roman settlement is only presumed to be Bath. From translation by G. K. Anderson.

⁴ Also *Exeter Book*. G. K. Anderson translation.

⁵ Another from *Exeter Book,* miscellaneous.

⁶ G. K. Anderson, trans.

⁷ Generally supposed to be the *Pearl* poet, author of *The Pearl, Patience,* and *Purity* (or *Cleanness*): the four poems are found in the same ms, Nero A. Cotton, vol. 4.

⁸ Only recently discovered. It contains an interesting autograph.

⁹ The English translation of which is usually attributed to Chaucer.

¹⁰ Canterbury Cathedral.

¹¹ In conjunction with religious festivals, esp. Corpus Christi.

¹² Though not the first secular drama, of course.

¹³ The first Italian to find political refuge in England, at the residence of the French ambassador. He remained from 1583 to 1585 and was burned at the stake at the Campo di Fiori (Rome) on February 17, 1600.

¹⁴ The first Folio, prepared by members of the company in 1623.

¹⁵ For King Duncan, read Banquo (*lapsus?*) (1.6.9).

[16] Admirably turned into Spanish by Manuel Mujica Láinez (au. notes).

[17] A political treatise in the form of a fable.

[18] From a Divine Sonnet (xiv).

[19] Tasso's discussion of choice of theme is presented in his *Discourse on the art of poetry,* where he recommends a Christian theme that is not concerned with unalterable articles of faith nor history too ancient. It is doubtful he would have approved of Milton's subject matter.

[20] This theory, among many, is known often as the Satanist fallacy.

[21] Reference is to the Ossian "Fragments" (1760) and "Fingal" (1762), etc., published by MacPherson. Their place in English literary history has declined, as the author elsewhere notes, but they are still considered important on the continent.

[22] The point—that Gibbon was a master of irony—is perhaps clearer in the Spanish text.

[23] Johnson was later to change his mind, recognizing that language is organic and cannot be fixed.

[24] Boswell put into practice theories of biography recommended, if not invented, by Johnson himself in various ways, though Johnson's own *Lives* seldom follow his theories. Boswell, thus, becomes the father of modern biography. The *Life* appeared in 1791, seven years after Johnson's death; the Spanish text says five years.

[25] The well-known Malahide Papers, etc., of which numerous volumes have appeared.

[26] Borges means *romantic* in the sense of nineteenth-century romantic movement.

[27] Lugones (1874–1938) was "Le plus grand poète d'Argentine," according to Van Tieghem's, *Histoire littéraire de l'Europe et de l'Amérique,* q.v.

[28] He recommends the language of common men.

[29] *The Excursion.*

[30] Published serially in *Fraser's Magazine,* 1833–1834.

[31] Macaulay's reputation has recently been at low ebb, perhaps sufficiently so to vitiate the comparison.

[32] In the sense of their influence on his own generation; "Sohrab and Rustum," "Scholar Gypsy," "Rugby Chapel," "Dover Beach," etc., are usually thought to be a major contribution.

[33] Somewhat as Frank Baum, to amuse a little girl named Dorothy Hall, wrote the *Wizard of Oz*.

[34] *Euclid and His Modern Rivals* (1879).

[35] "My life ended when I left the pampas," he claimed.

[36] Originally titled *The Purple Land That England Lost*.

[37] Though Blake was not always a follower of Swedenborg: of the latter's doctrine of predestination, as of Calvin's, Blake wrote, "cursed Folly!"

[38] Chilean poet, Nobel Prize 1972.

[39] From "Ulysses."

[40] With Holman Hunt, John Everett Millais, etc.

[41] *Poems* by D. G. Rossetti (1870), including "Sister Helen," "Eden Bower."

[42] *The House of the Wolfings, The Roots of the Mountains, The Wood Beyond the World,* etc. He considered the Kelmscott Press *Chaucer* (1894) his most important work.

[43] *"Ave atque Vale."*

[44] Published in R. L. S.'s collection *The Merry Men* (1887).

[45] Perhaps also *A Child's Garden of Verses*.

[46] *Poems* (1881) went through five editions in a year.

[47] Originally published in the *Scots Observer* and *English Illustrated Magazine;* collected with his *Departmental Ditties* and *Other Verse,* 1890.

[48] E.g., *The Outline of History, Short History of the World, The Science of Life* (with Julian Huxley and G. P. Wells).

[49] And novelist: he published four novels.

[50] "Creative Evolution," the title of one of his pamphlets. He also paradoxically recommended attending church.

[51] See his *De Divisione Naturalis,* where he expresses the principle of the unity of nature.

[52] Though he apparently always spoke English with an accent.

[53] *The Adventures of Sherlock Holmes* (1891); *The Memoirs of Sherlock Holmes* (1894), etc.

[54] Published as a fragment the year after James's death.

NOTES

[55] That is, the body in the locked room device so popular with mystery writers.

[56] *Lady Chatterley's Lover* was written three times. The authoritative version is the one privately printed in Florence in 1928; the earliest version titled *The First Lady Chatterley* was printed in 1944. There was also an expurgated version.

[57] According to F. R. Leavis in the *Great Tradition*.

[58] A private, somewhat shorter version appeared in 1922. First regular edition appeared only in 1935.

[59] And others (e.g., Joyce).

[60] Not in England, however, where *Mrs. Dalloway* and *To the Lighthouse* are probably better known.

[61] *James Joyce's Ulysses: A Study* (1931).

[62] J. Campbell and H. M. Robinson. An even better exposition is Edmund Wilson's chapter "The Dream of H. C. Earwicker" in *The Wound and the Bow* (1941).

[63] Also Spenser, Shelley, William Morris.